REPORT OF THE WORKING PARTY
CHAIRED BY
THE VERY REVEREND DR EDWARD CARPENTER
With Mrs Angela Bates, The Rev Trevor Beeson
Dr Michael Brambell, Prof Kenneth Carpenter
Mrs Lilian Carpenter, Mr David Coffey
Mrs Ruth Harrison, Prof Sydney Jennings
The Rev Andrew Linzey, The Rt Rev Dr Hugh Montefiore
Prof W H Thorpe

ANIMALS AND

ETHICS

WATKINS
London & Dulverton

ISBN: 0 7224 0180 9

Printed in Great Britain by A. Wheaton & Co. Ltd., Exeter

CONTENTS

*Note: the occasional repetition in this paper is deliberate,
being designed to make each main section self-contained.*

CHAIRMAN'S FOREWORD

This document is the product of a contemporary unease which fears that unless the onward march of technology, geared often to short term commercial interests, is made subject to scrutiny and effective overall control, the quality of life on this planet will be impoverished, not least when such technology is applied to our interaction with animals. This is a genuine concern felt acutely by serious minded and responsible people who are conscious of dangers ahead and are disturbed by the complacency with which these are too often regarded. This, of course, implies no criticism of the application, in itself, of the scientific method to ever increasing areas of human endeavour. Technology has a long and distinguished history going back to man's primitive efforts to bring an accession of power to his handling of his environment. Such an ambition is indeed older than the invention of the stone axe or the wheel. Without technology of some kind man could not live, and those who are most fearful of its present application are the first to recognise its many achievements and potential blessings.

The dangerous fallacy must, however, be exposed and rebuffed, namely that whatever *can* be done by deploying man's new found powers, derivative from the systematic investigation of nature, it is right for him to do unheeding of short or long term results. The ability and 'know how' to secure an end does not in itself give moral validity to that end. The exercise of such powers must be made to subserve worthwhile goals and morally tolerable satisfactions. This must mean that as science progressively moves on it cannot be left to work itself out at random or at the whim of separate, unrelated interests, many of them commercial. There must be guide-lines and overall planning directed towards the furtherance of valuable social objectives. Aristotle has it that society comes into existence that man may live: and continues in order that he may live well. So it is with technology. At a minimum level it is necessary if man is to live at all: it is now urgent that its fostering and continuance should be directed to man and not only man living well.

From such general thinking and presuppositions the environmental or ecological lobby has been formed. The literature around it is already considerable.

Animals and Ethics finds its place within the context of this overall environmental concern, though its writ is confined to that part of the environment represented by man's relations with, and control over, the animal species. It is here that responsible protests and informed criticisms are being voiced daily, not least because in many areas the injury done to animals and the impoverishment of their lives derives from the human will. In the nature of the case no suffering which animals endure in the supposed interests of mankind is self-chosen or vicariously undertaken for the good of the whole. Their plight, under contemporary economic pressures, has led, understandably, to an increasing animal lobby, varying in its composition, attitudes and interests.

In the view of those who have cooperated to produce this paper, it is both the psychological approach and the capacity born from technology which constitute the most serious menace to the animal creation. Sadistic drives in unregenerate man, leading to fitful cruelty, have always existed and will alas continue to do so. Their eradication demands a therapy better administered to the individual offender by the pastor and psychologist. While they exist and animals suffer as a consequence there must be legal restraint. More serious, and much more widespread, is a contemporary cruelty to animals operating in an institutionalised and structured form for which the whole community and not simply one section must in the last resort be held reponsible.

The overall aim of this paper is therefore to alert men of goodwill to a contemporary situation which by any showing is not a pleasant one. This document covers a wide field, so much so that it should be followed up in more specialised studies as indicated in the attached bibliography. Its main purpose is to stress the need for basic criteria by which to determine man's general attitude to animals in his diverse relations with them. Essential to the basic principles of such a relationship is that of a partnership between different orders of creation living side by side in the one world; also that of man as a steward, a trustee with special responsibilities vested in him. No effort has been made to romanticise either man or nature. The predatory character of both raises problems to the moral consciousness, which were ever present in the minds of the group. Opinions in this field, however, do not obtrude in this study. Common to all participants was a recognition of the need for a new 'reverence', a more sensitive feeling towards nature such that predominantly aggressive, manipulative techniques geared to exploitation and commercial gain do not take over.

The concern of this paper is with practical action and patterns of behaviour. The criteria suggested throughout this report need to be introduced into given situations, with the crunch question under honest and critical review - are there, sadly, circumstances in which the basic, essential, non-trivial needs of man ought to be given priority over the needs of animals - that is where both cannot be fully realised? This brings us to the heart of another and most serious problem - how, in practice, to resolve mutual and competing claims and how to balance respective 'goods' and 'evils'. This paper puts forward the thesis that in complex situations where no one authoritative judgement can be arrived at the animals should be given the benefit of the doubt. They cannot speak for themselves. Particularly is this the case with what looms large in the paper and is designated 'stress'. The inherent difficulty of applying only scientific criteria to detect its presence needs to be recognised. The judgement of the capable and experienced stockman is here not without importance.

Different readers of this study may well feel that it has erred too far in one direction or another. Some will doubtless complain that it lacks definition, that it does not sufficiently strike that clarion call of a challenge necessary to rally or fuel the forces of the animal lobby to the extent needed. We hope that this will not be the case, but if it is we would wish that those who feel this way will be motivated to translate the general principles here adumbrated into precise action, thus giving them a cutting edge and a proselytizing dynamic. Others may think that these same general principles ask too much of those commercially interested and if conscientiously applied would, by imposing upon them excessively severe restrictions, inhibit, indeed rule out, many contemporary practices. We can only hope that the principles will increasingly find acceptance and where necessary their application be written into enforceable legal codes of practice. For this to be brought about requires fact finding and objective surveys as well as insight and sensitivity.

INTRODUCTION

1 A group of biologists, theologians, veterinarians, and others concerned with the welfare of animals, met during 1977 - 1979 to prepare an agreed statement on man's relationship with animals which would reflect an ethical approach within a factual context.

2 Widespread unease in this area is currently felt by many thoughtful and responsible people as well as by active workers in animal welfare.

3 Man has always used animals to minister to his needs and in order to make human life easier. He makes them work for him, carry him, amuse him and gain financial rewards for him. He submits them to experiments in the hope that his own life will be longer, safer and more satisfying. He uses them as pets. He also uses them for food, clothing and many other purposes; indeed there is hardly a household which does not resort to animal products or by-products.

4 This usage of animals, particularly in the fields of scientific research and farming, raises serious and hitherto insufficiently explored ethical issues.

5 The fact is that the application of modern technology to ever increasing areas of human endeavour is enabling man to dominate his environment ever more completely, often to the detriment of animal life.

MAN'S STEWARDSHIP

6 Man has often used his power over animals in ways which revolt, and do violence to, his moral consciousness. On a theistic understanding of creation, such as the Christian entertains, it is misguided to suppose that all animal life exists only to serve human kind; or that the world was made exclusively for man's benefit. Man's estimate of his own supposed welfare should not be the only guideline in determining his relationship with other species.

7 In terms of this theistic understanding man is custodian of the universe he inhabits with no absolute rights over it. This implies a profound responsibility to deal with his environment in the light of his factual situation. This responsibility, therefore, extends not only to the betterment of his own but also to that of other species; and moreover to the interests of generations of both yet unborn.

8 There has been much discussion as to how far, and in what respect, animals have 'rights', and also precisely what the term 'rights' means in this context. Thus some theists would hold that animals, by reason of their divine creation, possess intrinsic rights. Others would prefer to say that animals should be regarded *as if* they had rights, such rights being accorded to them by man in his relationship with them. Holders of both views, however, would be in agreement that in practice animals should be treated with respect and dignity.

9 This principle should help to determine our dealings with animals; though like most principles it cannot be seen as absolutely binding in all circumstances. Indeed, in a world where predator and prey, host and parasite, are built into a competitive economy man is often forced to balance the relative claims of each species.

Thus we should not grant immunity to the tsetse fly leaving behind it a trail of sleeping sickness. In such situations of conflict we need to adopt reasoned moral criteria as a basis for practical action.

SIMILARITIES AND DIFFERENCES WITH MAN

10 There are important similarities and differences between men and animals, as in the degree of sentiency, the capacity for rational thought, the use of language, the degree of self-awareness, etc. There are also differences between different species in these and many other ways.

11 Above all and most imprtant, there is in man a highly developed moral consciousness which is possibly unique and which con-strains him to conceive moral ends and, if only fitfully, to pursue them. Such a consciousness imposes upon him a unique responsi-bility.

PAIN AND STRESS

12 The experience of stimulation and, on occasions, the stress which results from it, are part and parcel of organic life.

13 Man has the ability to investigate and observe behaviour patterns in the natural world and in these activities he cannot avoid using his own judgement to distinguish between levels of suffering where there is the capacity to experience it. He is biologically part of the animal world and is right, therefore, to assume that his experience of basic biological reactions differs mainly in degree from those of other animals. The nearer the animal to man in its evolutionary history (and the more primitive the cause of the suffering) the greater the likelihood of basic common experience in the bearing of pain, and in other sensations.

14 It becomes difficult and finally impossible to assess pain in the
    case of the lower invertebrate animals, such as, *inter alia*, the
    domestic cockroach, the garden slug, the earth-worm. On the
    other hand, in the higher vertebrate animals which are warm-
    blooded - birds, whales, mice, bats and all the large land animals
    (whether domesticated or wild) - there are very strong reasons
    evident in our immediate encounter with them for assuming
    the experience of something in animals which in ourselves we
    would regard as pain. Indeed man has to recognise that some
    animals are more sensitive to some types of stimulation than he
    is himself, (e.g. the ability of bats to hear very high frequency
    sound-waves, and of dogs to detect scents too faint to be smelled
    by man).

15 The assessment of stress is not without its difficulties. Never-
    theless (even without undue anthropomorphism) we find a vast
    amount of evidence that animals can suffer from stresses such
    as anxiety, boredom, discomfort, frustration and fear. Though
    animals and man can react with terror to present events there is
    little evidence that animals can anticipate the future and suffer
    the extreme foreboding terror to which man is liable. Never-
    theless animals may remember situations in which they were
    once in terror and show signs of dread when they are again in the
    same situation. Animals should be given the benefit of the doubt
    whenever possible.

MAN AND WILD ANIMALS

WILD ANIMALS WITH ONLY INDIRECT CONTACT WITH MAN

16 Much violence exists amongst and between animals. It is not for man to condemn this violence though it may perplex, distress and bemuse him. Man's responsibilities for the suffering of animals in the wild largely arise out of his own actions which interfere with the normal processes of wild life. The extent and outreach of man's technology and the vastness of his population mean that all forms of life on this planet are now affected by man, though some of the effects are too small or too remote for man to be able to assess or even to be aware of them.

17 Where man can recognise and assess the effects of his interference with wildlife he has a duty to consider the consequences of his actions and to take reasonable steps to lessen the interference where it is thought to be harmful. Though it is frequently argued that man himself is part of nature and his actions part of the natural process, we do not feel it is enough to let this argument stop at the destructive side of man's nature without accepting that his ability to analyse and adjust himself to the consequences of his actions is also part of nature.

18 It is prudent at this stage to distinguish the effect of man's actions on populations and types of wild organisms (the field of conservation in which man is inextricably bound, if only to preserve the quality of his environment for himself and succeeding generations) and the effects on individual animals.

ANIMALS IN THE WILD IN DIRECT CONTACT WITH MAN

19 Animals are capable of suffering. Much suffering occurs in animals in the natural order of things. It is the suffering caused directly and indirectly by man and the existence of which can be reasonably deduced and which could be reasonably avoided that ought to be the moral concern of man. It is also inevitable that man causes some suffering (ants underfoot; worms truncated by digging; rats, mice and bats dispossessed and worse by bulldozers and demolishers) but it would be unreasonable categorically to condemn walking or digging or bulldozing or demolition because of this. Man has been created too clumsy a creature to avoid the incidental hurting of other animals.

20 It is the infliction of avoidable suffering which is morally reprehensible. The moral difference between cruelty and causing suffering lies mainly in the motivation and awareness of the person inflicting the pain and not in the extent of the hurt caused to the sufferer. A lion disembowelling an antelope may cause far more suffering than the ill-aimed shot of the hunter, but only the hunter can be accused of cruelty. It is the wilful, deliberate infliction of suffering by man, or wanton action (without reasonable forethought and compassion) which constitutes cruelty. Cruelty implies a wrongly motivated conscious action by man, which causes pain for an end which in no way justifies it. It has to be said, however, somewhat casuistically, that the reduction of pain, no matter what the motive, is desirable.

21 The moral judgement of man in determining the extent of his interference with wild living animals must depend on achieving a balance between the reasonable needs of his own species and those of the animals.

22 Man interferes with living creatures in their wild environment in order to eat them, to remove their competition with himself, to observe them, to catch them in order to use them somewhere else and to kill them as a pastime. We feel that there is no moral prohibition against a responsible, discriminating, sensitive use of animals so long as there is no other way to secure the fundamental and real, as opposed to the superficial or trivial, benefit of man. We are acutely aware that judgements in the balancing of relative needs are largely subjective. We would hope that education, information, frank discussion, and insistence on right motivation will lead to sensitive appraisals of such situations. Nor ought we to relax efforts, through research, to discover alternative methods to secure the same ends.

23 Hunting to kill on land is now virtually restricted to aboriginal foodfinding, fur-trapping, 'pest'-control and pleasure-killing.

24 The methods used in hunting range from the bullet and lead shot, to traps, snares and nets. The suffering caused to the hunted animal varies from nil in the case of the well-stalked clean kill (though this does not, in every case, justify it), to prolonged distress in the case of the whale crippled by an explosive harpoon or the animal in an infrequently monitored snare. Here the moral propriety for man's action depends on the necessity to hunt, on the inherent hurtfulness of the method of hunting, and on the hunted animal's sensitivity to the stresses of hunting. Pleasure-killing seems to us to be lacking in moral justification and fur-trapping to have a weaker case than food finding. On the question of method it would appear that that which produces a quick death without a period of anxiety in the chase is more defensible than methods of a long drawn-out chase and slow death. On the question of sensitivity to suffering we can assume that there are different levels of awareness of danger; that deer and antelope sense danger sooner than frogs and toads; that

whales probably sense danger more quickly than do fish - indeed they may even be able to transmit their dread to each other in ways similar to man. We really have no grounds to suppose otherwise. Once in the throes of death it is not so clear that the whale or the deer have lower thresholds of pain than fish or frogs. However we feel that some animals are more likely to suffer foreboding, anxiety and terror than others. Pain ranges from the momentary prick to prolonged agony. The prick of a needle is as nothing compared with the explosion of a loaded harpoon and we are therefore of the opinion that to remove abuses it does not help for all suffering to be 'lumped' together as a great undesirable. What matters is that we use our judgement to assess the degree of suffering and that we always have a regard for the animal.

25 Man regards the species which interact with him to his detriment as pests. The fact that these species, such as rats and moles, are so regarded does not in any way imply that they have a higher threshold of pain than other species, and the same criteria of necessity, method and sensitivity should be applied to actions taken against them as are applied to species which he does not regard as pests.

WILD ANIMALS MANAGED BY MAN

26 We feel that the same criteria of necessity, method and sensitivity apply to man's control of the life of wild animals within his power as they do to those wild animals whose death is within his power. However, since the animals are being maintained alive for long periods (and perhaps even longer than their 'natural' life-span) there must be greater awareness of more subtle forms of suffering.

27 By controlling the life of an animal man is to some extent depriving the animal of the full range of its natural reactions to environmental stimuli. Removal from the wild may also deprive the animal of factors in its natural environment essential for its normal functioning; or in reverse introduce factors alien to such an environment which may prove equally detrimental. We do not argue that the 'natural' environment is necessarily the least stressful existence possible for all wild animals, (any more than it is for man himself) since nature can constitute a violent environment, but we do argue that to increase the stress is difficult to justify. Once man interferes we feel that he must at least ensure that stresses are no worse than those of the natural environment and that opportunities to avoid distress are at least equal to those in the wild. It is clear that animals adapt to their controlled living so that situations which could cause acute distress in the wild may cause little more than passing interest in captivity. We are not prepared to condemn the maintenance of wild animals in captivity as in all circumstances wrong. We recognise that a case can be made on educational and scientific grounds, on grounds of conservation and humanely conducted, discriminating experiments in some circumstances. We are satisfied that man may keep and use wild animals as part of his own pattern of life where there is a justifiable necessity; where the methods of capture, transport and maintenance are the least stressful available; and where the animals are entirely protected from persistent anguish, terror, pain and agony, and are able to live within normal ranges of environmental stimuli.

MAN AND MANAGED ANIMALS

28 Man's emergence from the primitive hunting phase which charac-
terised his pre-history existence meant that he became dependent
on his ability to domesticate plants and animals. Such ability
to control the environment of managed animals must entail
a direct responsibility for their welfare.

29 Welfare assessment is a notoriously difficult subject. Much of
it remains subjective. Members of this working group feel that
the welfare of any animal should be independent of its appeal
to man, its economic or extrinsic value. Certainly no system
should include environmental restrictions to provide trivial,
luxury items for man. Common welfare criteria must be applied
to all animals managed by man.

30 In the absence of evidence to the contrary, it is reasonable to
assume that the natural or wild environment to which animals
have adapted themselves through long years of evolution is
well suited to the demands of the species concerned. This does
not mean, however, that it is in all aspects essential. Even wild
animals may inhabit a variety of environments, since they are
able to adjust to environmental variation by employing behavioural and physiological mechanisms as fine tuners of adapta-
bility. Indeed adjustment to constantly changing environments
is normal.

31 We could wish that domestic or captive animals should be
allowed to express in all respects essential behavioural and
physiological possibilities rooted in their ancestral species.
The adaptive mechanisms which are available, however, within

limits, cope with some of the restrictive, even detrimental features of a domestic or captive existence. The welfare of managed animals is dependent upon the degree to which they can adapt without suffering to the environments provided by man.

32 So long as a species remains within the limits of the environmental range to which it can adapt without suffering, its well-being is assured. As it approaches the limits of its adaptive ability signs of stress appear. The signs exhibited will depend on the extent and nature of the environmental pressures. No common factor is identifiable. Animals may succumb to a massive single abuse or to a combination of smaller challenges each of which by itself would not prove disastrous. Also individual animals within one species react differently to the same external stimuli.

33 So far scientific method has, on balance, proved negative in providing criteria to assess welfare. It is necessary therefore, so long as this situation obtains, to adopt other criteria. Straddling the limits of adaptation and maladaptation is an area of unacceptable environmental stress. The problem is how the onset of these limits can be identified.

34 Anthropomorphism - that is judgements made by man arising out of his own subjective experience - is often thought of as scientifically suspect, though there is a sense in which all man's judgements are of this kind. There are, however, areas where its use is already considered respectable. The experience of pain is, of course, totally subjective, but it is not unreasonable for a person to infer from his own experience the signs of its presence in others, and this includes animals. Neither is an 'island'. It is surely not unreasonable to make similar assessments when dealing with other aspects of animal welfare. There are

behavioural and socio-physiological limits beyond which observation of an animal indicates that it begins to experience distress and suffering. The identification of these limits where scientific criteria are inadequate is clearly subjective but they are not therefore rightly ignored or written off.

35 The number and variety of species managed by man are legion. The spectrum extends from collections of wild animals in zoological parks to the very intensive systems found in modern agriculture, and includes animals kept as pets and for experimental purposes.

36 Diligent human care for the welfare of such animals as are confined in a few advanced zoological parks can act as a touchstone for the welfare standards of managed animals. The concern of those responsible for these institutions is to provide an environment without distress. The welfare of the animal is of paramount importance. We accept that such an extremely favourable situation is not always possible in otherwise well managed animals since interference with their natural inclinations is an intrinsic feature of their domestic or captive existence. Here the line between the permissible and impermissible must be drawn and the animal given the benefit of the doubt.

BASIC GUIDELINES

37 Certain basic guidelines should govern the management of animals under the direct control of man. No husbandry method should deny the environmental requirements of the basic behavioural needs of these animals. These needs will include the following:
- freedom to perform natural physical movement
- association with other animals, where appropriate of their own kind

- facilities for comfort activities, e.g. rest, sleep and body care
- provision of food and water to maintain full health
- ability to perform daily routines of natural activities
- opportunity for the activities of exploration and play, especially
    for young animals
- satisfaction of minimal spatial and territorial requirements
    including a visual field and 'personal' space.

Deviations from these principles should be avoided as far as possible, but where such deviations are absolutely unavoidable efforts should be made to compensate the animal environmentally.

THE ANIMALS MAN USES FOR FOOD

THE NEED

38 Plant foods can feed many times more people when they are fed direct to human beings than when they are fed through animals. Since there is only a limited amount of agricultural land on our planet to provide food for all its inhabitants, the extent to which livestock can be incorporated into farming systems must depend upon the amount of land available for the grazing of livestock and for growing feed-stuffs, after basic food needs have been met.

39 Man can achieve a nutritionally adequate diet without animal-products provided he has available to him a sufficiency and variety of suitable plant-foods. In many regions of the world, however, he depends on limited amounts of animal-products, especially dairy-produce, to balance his diet. In a few limited areas, such as Alaska, dependence on animal-foods is heavy.

40 Man's domestication of food-animals goes back over many thousands of years and he has become accustomed to using more and more animal-products to make his diet more varied and luxurious. The degree to which this has been taken in the richer countries goes far beyond even the most generous inter-pretation of need. This being so, man can clearly afford to be more generous in the methods he uses for rearing livestock than is often the case today.

METHODS

41 There are very wide variations in livestock systems. At one
    extreme are those such as the hill farming of sheep and cattle
    in which the animals roam freely over vast acreages and only
    see the inside of a building when they reach the slaughterhouse;
    at the other extreme are the highly-automated systems of close
    confinement in which almost the only time the animal sees
    daylight or the outside of a building is when it is taken out
    on the way to slaughter. Between these two extremes there is
    every conceivable gradation. The greater man's control over the
    animal the greater, by and large, will be the interference with
    its natural inclinations.

42 We recognise the important part that good stockmanship (an
    inherent feeling for the animal) and good management (attention
    to detail) can play in contributing to the welfare of farm
    animals. But although a high standard of stockmanship and
    management can prevent further suffering in an inherently poor
    system and, conversely, bad mangement and poor stockmanship
    can be the cause of suffering in a basically sound system, we
    feel that the aim must be for sound systems which are both
    well-managed and with good stockmen.

43 During the last twenty years economic pressures have forced
    farmers on a limited acreage to meet rising costs by increasing
    profits and one way of doing this has been to increase livestock
    numbers. As livestock numbers have increased so has the cor-
    responding investment in research. The research has led to more
    productive strains of animal, to a far greater knowledge of the
    animal's nutritional and environmental needs and of the diagnosis
    and treatment of disease. However, the routine prophylactic
    use of antibiotics and other drugs has made it possible to

intensify the population of animals in each building to an extent which would previously have proved disastrous; and this has led to a move away from mixed farming and towards specialisation not only in one species but even in one form of production.

44 During this period there has been a steady drift of labour away from the land, and manufacturers in allied industries have concentrated their innovative skills on maximising the use of their own products in equipment and gadgetry geared to ease of management. Specialised buildings with standardised pens, stalls or cages, lend themselves to automation and this has reached sophisticated levels not only covering such things as feeding, watering and slurry-removal, but also lighting, ventilation and temperature-control. The design of systems has thus moved out of the hands of traditional stockmen and into the hands of engineers and technicians, men of great skill and ingenuity but usually with little knowledge of animals, and in particular of animal behaviour. Whereas in the early days of automation it was thought that the stockman would, by being saved time on routine chores such as feeding, watering and dung-removal, have more time to care for the animals, in practice the reverse has happened. Less time spent on chores means that more animals can be taken on and overall productivity increased; the greater the number of mass-production techniques employed the greater the alienation of the stockman from his stock and the more rigidly the animal has to conform as one of a mass to the dictates of gadgetry and fashion regardless of its individual powers of adaptation.

45 Within the systems of extreme confinement in Britain we now have *inter alia* around forty-five million laying-hens kept in crowded battery-cages, unable to spread even one wing and standing permanently on sloping wire-mesh; around half a million sows kept in narrow stalls in which they are unable to

turn round, standing on open-grid flooring or on an unbedded floor of concrete; and some tens of thousands of young calves, destined for the 'white-veal' market, kept in slatted-floored crates, unable to turn round, unable to lie down freely, or even freely to groom themselves. All these animals may be in darkened buildings as an antidote to restlessness, aggressiveness or the abnormal behaviour to which such conditions give rise. Some of the mutilations carried out on farm animals, such as the tail-docking of pigs and the de-beaking of chickens, are used for the same purpose.

DISCUSSION

46 An animal is an animal. When animal-life is under man's control he has a responsibility to provide its basic welfare-needs regardless of the use to which it is put. The basic welfare-needs of the calf or piglet are neither quantitatively nor qualitatively different from those of a puppy or kitten; the welfare of farm-animals is assured only so long as the environment provided by man is not outside its ability to adapt without suffering.

47 As stated previously, it is reasonable to assume in the absence of evidence to the contrary that the natural or wild environment to which animals have adapted by the evolutionary process is well suited to the species concerned, and should be used as a basis for assessing the environment to be provided by man. Animals are able to adjust to a wide variety of environments, but as a species approaches the limits of its adaptive ability signs of maladaptation appear. Straddling the limits of adaptation and maladaptation is an area of unacceptable environmental stress.

48 Man is himself part of the animal world - his physiology, anatomy and basic behaviour is shared with animals. He can assume, therefore, that his experience of basic biological reactions differs

only in degree from those of other animals. When he has an intimate contact with an animal he can distinguish many degrees of stress, comparable to human anxiety, boredom, discomfort, frustration, foreboding and fear, and he can only infer that these exist also in animals with which he is not so intimate. The well-being of an animal which is permitted to exercise its inherent behaviour - for example, a pig rooting, a calf ruminating, a hen dust- bathing, a young animal at play - is often evident to the unbiased observer, incontrast to the animal which is prevented from carrying out these activities but making every effort to do so. The fact that it is difficult to demonstrate under controlled laboratory conditions the precise instinctive behaviour-patterns or emotional needs of an animal should not be used as an excuse for abandoning the attempt to provide an environment in which as many as possible of these natural behaviour-patterns can be expressed. Here again the animal should be given the benefit of the doubt wherever possible.

49 Whilst man cannot escape from exploiting other animals it is the degree to which this is taken that is important. Livestock-farming should not be purely an industrial process divorced from the land. In general terms a species should only be kept where conditions are suited to that species, for example pigs on light, well-drained soil on which they can root.

50 Diligent human care for the welfare of such animals as are confined in a few advanced zoological parks can act as a touchstone for the welfare standards of these managed animals. The concern of those responsible is to provide an environment without distress. The welfare of the animal is of paramount importance. We accept that such an extremely favourable situation is not always possible since a measure of interference with its natural inclinations is an intrinsic feature of domestic or captive existence. Here the line between the permissible and imper-

missible must be drawn.

51 The basic guidelines set out earlier should govern the management of farm animals. No husbandry system should deny the environmental requirements of their basic behavioural needs. These include the following:
 - freedom to perform natural physical movement
 - association with other animals, where appropriate of their own kind
 - facilities for comfort-activities, e.g. rest, sleep and body care
 - provision of food and water to maintain full health
 - ability to perform daily routines of natural activities
 - opportunity for the activities of exploration and play, especially for young animals
 - satisfaction of minimal spatial and territorial requirements including a visual field and 'personal' space.
Deviations from these principles should be avoided as far as possible, but where such deviations are absolutely unavoidable efforts should be made to compensate the animal environmentally.

52 It is clear that a number of systems presently used do not satisfy these criteria, amongst which are hen-batteries, veal-crates and sow-stalls.

THE ANIMALS MAN USES AS PETS

THE NEED

53 As far as we know man has always lived in a state of interdependence with animals and formed symbiotic relationships with particular species and this is the origin of the modern domestication of animals. But we can find no parallel to the modern, almost universal, use of many other species as pets.

54 Man's use of animals as pets is designed to realise two overlapping purposes - to fulfil practical needs, such as guide-dogs for the blind, and companionship. In the latter category animals can fulfil one or more of the following functions - again overlapping; education in the school or home; the psychological need for affection or even recompense for the loss of it; as a status symbol; the fulfilment of a competitive instinct of some kind, or the desire to possess and control.

55 Never before in human society has there been such a wide range of pets kept to satisfy personal and emotional needs. We have become accustomed to regard as normal the keeping of pets under a great variety of circumstances and the practice is seldom questioned. Pet-ownership has become a common facet of social and family life.

SOME OF THE PROBLEMS

56 *Abuses:* The lavish and almost indiscriminate use of animals as pets results in much abuse. Apart from acts of deliberate

cruelty there are many areas of abuse including neglect, abandon-
ment, over-indulgence, mutilation, and the keeping of animals
in conditions entirely unsuited to their species (especially exotic
animals). There are also areas of concern in the industries dealing
with the breeding and marketing of pets.

57 *Population:* An over-lavish pet-population is socially and finan-
cially costly, wasteful of food-resources, and the cause of environmental pollution. Pet-keeping on the scale reached today
has never been properly evaluated with regard to: (i) global food-
resources; (ii) the destruction of other species used for pet-food,
such as whales, kangaroos and horses, and (iii) the social and
environmental costs, possible health-hazards, nuisance-problems,
and so on.

58 *Commercial usage:* The use of animals as pets is promoted and
exploited in many different ways:
   i)   through direct trade in animals in shops and markets;
   ii) by the allied industries servicing pet-keeping, such as
        those involved in the production and manufacture of
        foodstuffs, drugs, equipment and luxury items;
   iii) by those involved with the competitive breeding and
        showing of pet animals, and
   iv) by dealers in exotic pets such as tortoises, reptiles, birds
        and monkeys.

CONTROL

59 There is a lack of any overall control of the pet-populations.
Indeed no adequate statistics are kept which would enable the
recording of the number and variety of such animals. Where a
licensing system is in being, as for dogs in Britain, it is unen-
forced, inadequate and ineffectual. There has been a proliferation of animal-shelters and sanctuaries in recent years providing

varying degrees of care. Furthermore we have come to accept, as a society, the mass destruction of millions of unwanted animals each year, often by questionable methods.

CONCLUSIONS

60 In view of the above, the disadvantages to both animals and humans of widespread pet-keeping need to be carefully balanced against many of the assumed advantages. We cannot accept that people have the inalienable right to use animals as pets under any circumstances. We believe it to be dehumanising as well as immoral to keep pet animals subject to many of the conditions in which they are kept today - even by 'animal lovers'.

61 We do not deny, however, that in many situations, provided that the correct environmental conditions prevail and there is real respect for the well-being of the animal concerned, pet owner-ship can be a fulfilling experience. The clue to successful management of domestic pets lies in an understanding of their needs. Over-indulgence and over-protectiveness can be as detrimental to their welfare as is blatant cruelty.

62 *We recommend that:*
    a) anyone contemplating having a pet animal must accept that the responsibility will last throughout the life of that animal and he must make himself aware of the animal's needs *before* obtaining it. If he parts with the animal the transfer must be undertaken responsibly;
    b) consideration should be given as to whether the home circumstances provide a suitable environment for the species concerned. Paradoxically, it is just those who live in 'concrete jungles', where the atmosphere is so hostile to both man and animal alike, who feel the greatest need for pets in order to maintain some sort of contact with nature. We

feel, however, that very few animals can adapt to living in flats or houses without gardens or ready access to open spaces, and that animals such as dogs, which depend on man for companionship, exercise and variety of activity, should not be owned by people who are out at work all day or frequently away from home. Consideration should also be given to the financial aspect of pet ownership, and the restrictions and inconveniences to the family weighed against the attractions and pleasures;

c) the basic guidelines governing the welfare of other animals managed by man should also apply to pet animals. (see 37)

d) that education in pet-ownership and the fostering of practical measures for responsible pet-ownership should be accepted as one of the important tasks facing society.

63 We believe that a responsible attitude to the keeping of pets will result in a substantial reduction in their number with a corresponding improvement in the welfare of those which remain. We find the continued uncontrolled breeding and sale of pets, which ignores the eventual and inevitable destruction of so many of them, unacceptable.

64 We believe that the importation, direct from the wild, of exotic species for use as pets should cease. Any trade which involves an inevitable cost in animal life and suffering, and which encourages the keeping of animals in totally unsuitable environments should not be allowed.

65 Finally, with pet animals - as with other managed animals - to cause any animal needless suffering is a betrayal of our moral responsibility to them as creatures wholly dependent upon us.

THE ANIMALS MAN USES
IN RESEARCH

THE NEED

66 Animals are used in research (i) in order to further the solution
of a human problem, (ii) in order to further the solution of
an animal problem, or (iii) for other scientific or technological
purposes.

67 There are many Acts of Parliament which require testing to be
performed on living animals. Some of those in force in Britain,
for example, are:
Agriculture (Poisonous Substances) Act, 1952 which gives
protection to agricultural workers from toxic substances used
in their work.
Food and Drugs Act, 1955 covering food and food additives.
The Medicines Act, 1968 which ensures that all medicinal substances, both prophylactic and therapeutic, for human and
veterinary use, are both efficacious and safe. Safety covers
toxicity, carcinogenicity, teratogenicity, and the effect on
reproduction.
The Health and Safety at Work Act, 1974 whilst not stipulating
the actual use of animals, will undoubtedly add to the number
of animals used in research. It makes it 'the duty of any person
who manufactures, imports or supplies any substance for use
at work to ensure so far as is reasonably practicable that the
substance is safe and without risks to health when properly
used.'

68 It is also pertinent to note that a programme for human protection drawn up in the EEC, and adopted by the Council of
Ministers in 1975, requires protection for consumers on a wide
range of products not all of which are covered in the above
Acts, such as cosmetics, detergents, consumer-durables, textiles,
toys, dangerous substances, and objects coming into contact
with foodstuffs.

69 The great increase in claims for damages made against manufacturers and government when ill health or disability arise due
to contact with a particular substance probably also gives rise
to an excess of caution involving more research on animals than
would otherwise be the case.

70 Commercial competition leads firms to market new products
differing only minutely in formula from the old, but because
of the change in formula they require testing on animals. This
also inevitably leads to far more animals being used than if such
competition were somehow brought under control. The World
Health Organisation has produced a list containing 200 drugs
essential for health. 2,000 drugs are marketed annually in Britain.

CONFLICTING RESPONSIBILITIES

71 We are in a world in which the different species are mutually
dependent and depend on common biosystems. This interdependence is a cardinal feature of the natural world - which
of course includes man. He cannot, therefore, hold himself
aloof. His dependence upon other species, whilst of course not
wrong in itself, always carries with it the danger of over-exploita-
tion and it is therefore the motives, means and ends of such
exploitation which man, as a responsible, rational being, must
consider.

72 We accept the principle that within this context of man's dependence upon other species it is wrong to be the cause of avoidable ill. We further accept that avoidability will be differently understood according to circumstances, needs and available technological knowledge.

73 Man is in a most unhappy predicament, torn between conflicting responsibilities. On the one hand he has a responsibility not to inflict avoidable ill on others, and on the other a responsibility to work towards the prevention and relief of suffering both in his own species and in the animals under his control.

74 Ironically, the greater the degree of protection man demands for himself from all the possible hazards with which he may be faced during his varied activities, the greater will be the pressure to ensure his safety through yet more and more experiments on animals.

75 Many fundamental and complex questions arise to which answers must be sought, chief among which are:
   i)   where does discomfort end and pain and distress begin?
   ii) is it right to conduct experiments on animals which cause them pain?
   iii) if it is, how far is the infliction of pain or distress permissible in the interests of:
        a) other animals?
        b) human beings?
        c) the advancement of knowledge?
   iv) what distinctions should be drawn between experiments which ensure the safety of:
        a) an adult user?
        b) a child?
        c) an unborn child?
It is not easy to find simple answers to these questions.

76 There are other wider issues relevant to the above, the importance of which we cannot emphasise too strongly, and which
we feel are not sufficiently discussed. Basic to the question of
the validity of experiments is the type of society man actually
wants and the cost to himself of achieving it. Do we as a society,
for example, really want research to be continued into such
devastating ways of killing our fellows as those envisaged in
biological weapons of warfare? Are there any ills we are prepared
to bear rather than resort to experiments on animals? Are we,
for example, through blind obedience to 'technological progress'
continuing to create problems that perpetuate the necessity for
animal experimentation, or are we actively creating a society
in which the necessity for experiments on animals will be drastically reduced? Have enough enthusiasm and effort - enough
real interest - gone into planning for happiness and health, and
into educating the public into healthier ways of living and eating?
We would like to see as much effort put into preventing ill
health and stress as is now put into mitigating its ill-effects.

MANAGEMENT

77 As important as the question of the necessity of experimentation
on animals is a consideration of their management in laboratories
and institutions before and after as well as during experimental
periods.

78 Although the conditions under which laboratory animals are
kept has improved over the years it is still common practice
to keep many of the animals in small pens or cages which permit
little exercise and provide a minimum of environmental stimuli.

79 Common welfare criteria must be applied to all animals under
the complete control of man and this includes laboratory animals
kept for research as much as any other animals kept outside

their natural environment.

80 The same basic guidelines should govern the conditions under which these animals are kept as for other managed animals. No husbandry method should deny the environmental requirements of the basic behavioural needs of these animals. These needs will include the following:
- freedom to perform natural physical movement
- association with other animals, where appropriate of their own kind
- facilities for comfort-activities, e.g. rest, sleep and body-care
- provision of food and water to maintain full health
- ability to perform daily routines of natural activities
- opportunity for the activities of exploration and play, especially for young animals
- satisfaction of minimal spatial and territorial requirements including a visual field and 'personal' space.

Deviations from these principles should be avoided as far as possible but where such deviations are absolutely unavoidable efforts should be made to compensate the animal environmentally.

81 *We recommend:*
   i)   A more intensified drive to find alternatives to the use of animals for research.
   ii) More careful thought about experiments before undertaking those involving the use of animals, including consideration of whether the object of the experiment is likely to be achieved by the method used.
   iii) Before embarking on a project entailing the use of animals, a research worker should satisfy himself that no alternative technique (e.g. cell-culture) will meet the need of his investigation.
   iv) Those engaged in experimentation on animals must ask

themselves, in considering the ethical justification of a given
project, whether the end to be realised is sufficiently signi-
ficant to warrant such infliction of pain and stress as might
be involved. This question, and it is a serious one, cannot be
ignored, and a given presupposition for the answering of it
must be that the animal should be treated as if it possesses
rights.

v) Where the use of animals, after these safeguards have been
taken, is regarded as necessary, careful thought should be
given to deciding the number that will be required. Some
species may be more appropriate than others in a given
instance, either because the nearest approximation to man
is a primary consideration, or because of a known specificity
of response in a particular species or strain. At this stage
economic considerations should not be paramount and
scientifically appropriate species should be selected; the use
of rare species should be avoided. In planning the number
of investigations to be performed, care should be taken to
limit the series to the minimum compatible with statistically
valid results.*

vi) Only animals from recognised breeding establishments
should be used and these should be subject to the same
management criteria as for other animals managed by man
(see 77-80 above). This would not only cut down on the
suffering - and high mortality - inherent in the capture and
transport of wild animals; it would also make a contribution
towards cutting down on the animals needed in that variations due to environmental factors would be minimised.

vii) Animals in research-establishments should be under the
permanent care of a veterinary surgeon and in particular
those having undergone surgery should receive constant
care and supervision.

viii)There should be discontinuation of experimentation for
trivial purposes, e.g. for luxury goods such as adornment

articles (there are already sufficient of these articles available to satisfy any actual need). Experiments designed to prove the obvious should be discontinued. There should also be discontinuation of animal research into products such as tobacco which man continues to take in full consciousness of the hazards of so doing.

ix) In view of the moral issues involved we recommend a more detailed investigation of the ethical considerations than was possible in this brief summary.

x) Greater efforts should be made at the retrieval of existing information on a world-wide basis to prevent unnecessary duplication.

xi) It should be generally accepted that only a person who has the requisite skill and understanding to prevent unnecessary suffering should undertake research, (particularly that involving surgery).

xii) Editors of scientific journals should refuse to publish papers where the research has necessitated manifestly inhumane experiments on animals.

xiii)There should be legal control over the proliferation arising from commercial competition of products which require testing on experimental animals.

* (iii) and (v) are taken from notes prepared by the Royal College of Surgeons for the guidance of research workers.

SUMMARY AND CONCLUSIONS

82 In our world the different species are completely interdependent and it is clear that none can have absolute rights. Nor can man, even if he so wished, avoid all exploitation of other species. It is, therefore, the degree and the avoidability of our exploitation which is our moral concern.

83 The degree of suffering experienced by an animal is dependent on its own physiological and anatomical make-up and is totally unrelated to its beauty, its rarity, its economic or its nuisance value. The welfare of the animal must therefore be considered independently of these things.

84 Common welfare-criteria must be applied to all animals managed by man.

85 Man is himself part of the animal world, his physiology, anatomy and basic behaviour are shared with the higher animals. He can assume, therefore, that his experience of basic biological reactions differs only in degree from those of other animals.

86 In the absence of evidence to the contrary, it is reasonable to assume that the natural or wild environments to which animals have adapted by the evolutionary process are well suited to the demands of the species concerned. This does not mean that they are indispensable. Even wild animals may inhabit a variety of environments. Animals managed by man should, as far as possible, be allowed to express all forms of behavioural and physiological potential available to the wild or ancestral species; where they are inhibited in any way the inhibition must be

seen as necessary to promote a worthwhile end.

87 The welfare of managed animals relates to the degree to which
   they can adapt without suffering to the environments designated
   by man. So long as a species remains within the limits of the
   environmental range to which it can adapt, its well-being is
   assured.

88 There are basic guidelines, respecting the dignity of the animal,
   which should govern the management of any animals managed
   by man. These, as previously stated, seek to ensure that no
   husbandry-method will deny the environmental requirements
   of the basic behavioural needs of the animals. These needs will
   include the following:
   - freedom to perform natural physical movement
   - association with other animals, where appropriate of their
      own kind
   - facilities for comfort activities, e.g. rest, sleep and body-care
   - provision of food and water to maintain full health
   - ability to perform daily routines of natural activities
   - opportunity for the activities of exploration and play, especially
      for young animals
   - satisfaction of minimal spatial and territorial requirements
      including a visual field and 'personal' space.
   Deviations from these principles should be avoided as far as
   possible, but where such deviations are absolutely unavoidable
   efforts should be made to compensate the animals environmentally.

89 Although different members of the group did not entirely
   agree on the degree of exploitation they felt to be acceptable,
   they did all agree that curbs were necessary in the exploitation
   of wild animals and in the three other areas of exploitation
   specifically detailed in this report: the animals man uses as food,

as pets, and in research.

90 Of especial concern is the application of scientific technology where this is detrimental to animal life. The ability and 'know-how' to secure an end does not in itself give validity for that end. The exercise of such powers must be made to subserve worthwhile goals and morally tolerable satisfactions.

91 This paper puts forward the thesis that in complex situations where no authoritative judgement can be made the animals should be given the benefit of the doubt. They cannot speak for themselves.

(i) *Food animals:* Plant foods can feed many-times more people when they are fed direct to human beings than when they are fed through animals. Since there is only a limited amount of agricultural land on our planet to provide food for all its inhabitants, the extent to which livestock can be incorporated into farming-systems on cultivated farm-land must depend upon the amount of land available after basic food needs have been met, for the grazing of livestock and for growing feeding-stuffs. Man's consumption of animals and animal-products goes far beyond even the most generous interpretation of need particularly in richer countries. Man can therefore clearly afford to be more generous in the methods he uses for rearing livestock than is often the case today.

The application of our basic guidelines would preclude in their present form many of the systems, such as commercial battery-cages, sow-stalls and veal-crates, currently in use.

(ii) *Pet animals:* Never before in human society has there been such a wide range of pets kept for personal and emotional needs. The disadvantages to both animals and humans of widespread pet-keeping need to be carefully balanced against many of the assumed advantages.

We believe that our recommendations would lead to more knowledgeable and responsible pet ownership, to a substantial reduction in the number and types of pets kept, and to the virtual elimination of the large-scale destruction of pet animals common today.

(iii) *Research animals:* Man is in a most unhappy predicament, torn between conflicting responsibilities. On the one hand he has a responsibility not to inflict avoidable harm on others, and on the other a responsibility to work towards the prevention and relief of suffering both in his own species and in the animals under his control.

Ironically, the greater the degree of protection man demands for himself from all the possible hazards he may face during his varied activities, the greater will be the pressure to ensure his safety through yet more experiments on animals and hence a proliferation of laws compelling further experimentation.

Whilst there are no answers to the many fundamental questions which arise concerning this use of animals we do feel that there is little justification for some of the uses and that some of the legal requirements lead to an unnecessary escalation of experiments.

The adoption of our recommendations would lead to a substantial drop in the number of animals used, the application of our basic guidelines to an improvement in the lives of animals used in research and to the preclusion of some experimental procedures.

92 There are certain practices which members of the group thought to be entirely inconsistent with the guidelines of this report - in particular:

i) Pleasure killing in all its forms.

ii) Research which uses animals for testing non-essential articles such as adornment articles (sufficient of these products are already in existence for any essential purposes); experiments designed to prove the obvious; research into products, such as tobacco, which man often continues to take in full consciousness of the hazards involved.

iii) Entertainment which centres around the suffering of animals, such as dog-fighting, rodeos, and some of the uses of animals in films.

iv) The use of certain livestock systems (see 91), and

v) The importation direct from the wild of exotic animals to be used as pets. (see 64).

93 When does society say 'enough is enough'? Basic to the answering of this question is a consideration of the type of society we actually want and the cost to ourselves of actually achieving it. Also, beyond this, we should ask whether there are any ills we humans are prepared to bear or risks we should take rather than alleviate them by experiments on animals. Are we ready to forego a lavish use of meat and animal-products in order that animals can enjoy more pleasant lives and in the hope that the world's resources may be more equitably distributed? Are we to continue to create problems that perpetuate the necessity for animal experimentation through blind obedience to technological 'progress'? Or do we wish actively to create a society in which such practices will be drastically reduced and, it is hoped, progressively eliminated? Has as much effort and enthusiasm gone into planning for health, happiness and harmonious co-existence as is now put into mitigating the effects of ill-health and stress and the satisfaction of our every whim?

94 A guiding principle, implied throughout this paper, is that adumbrated by Schweitzer: 'Reverence for Life'. Its application to given situations may on occasions present difficulties, but we

believe it is the right moral approach. It requires that when one life is impaired or sacrificed in the interests of another it can only be done responsibly, regretting that such situations should ever arise. Reverence implies respect; it ascribes dignity; it eschews the wanton and it abominates the cruel.

Carpenter, E.F.- *Common Sense about Christian Ethics*, Gollancz, 1961 *

Clark, Kenneth - *Animals and Man*, Thames and Hudson, 1977

Coffey, D. - *Encyclopaedia of Cats and Cat Care*, David and Charles, 1975 *

Fraser, A.F. - *Farm Animal Behaviour*, Bailliere Tindall, 1974, 2nd Ed 1980

Godlovitch, R.and S. and Harris, J.(eds.) - *Animals, Men and Morals* Gollancz, 1971

Harrison, Ruth - *Animal Machines*, Vincent Stuart, 1964*

Hedliger, H. - *Man and Animal in the Zoo*, Routledge and Kegan Paul, 1969

Hume, C.W. - *The Status of Animals in the Christian Religion*, Universities Federation for Animal Welfare, 1957

Jordan, W.J. and Ormrod, S. - *The Last Great Wild Beast Show*, Constable, 1978

Linzey, Andrew - *Animal Rights*, SCM Press, 1976 *

Montefiore, Hugh (ed.) - *Man and Nature*, Collins, 1975 *

Niall, Ian - *Around My House*, Heinemann, 1973

Pratt, Dallas - *Painful Experiments on Animals*, Argus Archives, 1976

Singer, P. - *Animal Liberation*, Jonathan Cape, 1975

Smyth, D.H. - *Alternatives to Animal Experiments*, Scholar Press, 1978

Schweitzer, A. - *My Life and Thought*

Thorpe, W.H. - *Animal Nature and Human Nature*, Methuen, 1974 *

Tudge, Colin - *The Famine Business*, Faber & Faber, 1977

Turner, E.S. - *All Heaven in a Rage*, Michael Joseph, 1964

Veselovsky, Dr. Z. - *Are Animals Different?*, Methuen, 1973

Reports, Papers, etc.

'Charter of Man's Duty Towards Animals', World Federation for the Protection of Animals, 1974

'Codes of Recommendations for the Welfare of Livestock', Report of the Farm Animal Welfare Advisory Committee, M.A.F.F., 1970

Hume, C.W. 'What Rights have Animals?', paper read to the Cambridge University Circle of the Newman Society, U.F.A.W., 1959

Hume, C.W. 'In Praise of Anthropomorphism', paper read to the Association for the Study of Animal Behaviour, U.F.A.W., 1959

'Man in his Living Environment', Report of a Working Party commissioned by the Board for Social Responsibility, C.I.O., 1970

'Report of the Departmental Committee on Experiments on Animals', Cmnd. 2641, HMSO, 1965

'Report of the Technical Committee to enquire into the Welfare of Livestock kept under Intensive Husbandry Systems', Cmnd. 2836, HMSO, 1970 reprint.

'Socio-ethical Requirements for the Protection of Animals', Institute of Social Ethics, Zurich.

Report of the Working Party on Dogs, Department of the Environment, HMSO, 1975.

* see other publications in biographical notes

Members of the Working Party

THE VERY REV. DR. EDWARD CARPENTER (Chairman) Dean of Westminster. President, World Congress of Faiths, Modern Churchman's Union, Anglican Society for the Welfare of Animals; Vice-Chairman, R.S.P.C.A. Chairman, Religious Advisory Committee of the United Nations; Joint Chairman, London Society of Jews and Christians. Publications: *Common Sense about Christian Ethics* (1961); *The Service of a Parson* (1965); *Cantuar* (1971); *Man of Christian Action* (1976); (ed.) *House of Kings* (1966); contrib. *Man in his living environment* (1970).

MRS. ANGELA BATES Working director of Vitrition Limited (premixes and advice on animal feeds). Runs large pig-farm. Member, Government's Farm Animal Welfare Council. Vice-President, Soil Association.

THE REV. TREVOR BEESON Canon and Treasurer, Westminster Abbey. Former Editor, *New Christian*. Currently European Editor, *Christian Century*. Publications: *The Crisis in the Church of England* (1970); *Discretion and Valour* (1973); *Britain: Today and Tomorrow* (1979).

DR. MICHAEL BRAMBELL Director, North of England Zoological Society (Chester Zoo); formerly Curator of Mammals, Zoological Society, London. Chairman, Scientific Authority for Animals (advises Sec. of State for Environment on working of Washington Convention to Control International Trade in Endangered Species; former Chairman, Library Committee of the Linnaean Society of London. Publications: *Horses, Tapirs and Rhinoceroses* (1976); contrib. *Breeding Endangered Species in Captivity* (1975); *International Zoo Yearbook* (1968 -); many scientific papers, incl. *The Management of Young Mammals* (1977); and *Reintroduction* (1977).

PROFESSOR KENNETH CARPENTER Prof. Experimental Nutrition, University of California, Berkeley; formerly Fellow of Sidney Sussex College, Reader in Nutrition, University of Cambridge.

MRS. LILIAN CARPENTER married to the Dean of Westminster. Graduated Guildhall School of Music and Drama. Actively involved in animal welfare.

MR. DAVID COFFEY Veterinary surgeon in general practice. Formerly with Bahamas Humane Society, Blue Cross in London, Ministry of Agriculture as Research Officer studying animal behaviour, Scientific Assessor to the Minister's Farm Animal Welfare Advisory Committee. Publications: *Encyclopaedia of Cats and Cat Care* (1975); *Encyclopaedia of Sea Mammals* (1977); *Encyclopaedia of Aquarium Fish* (1977). Contrib. Scientific journals.

MRS. RUTH HARRISON Member of Government's Farm Animal Welfare Council and Council Member of World Federation for Protection of Animals. Publications include *Animal Machines* (1964), which led to setting up of Brambell Committee in same year; contrib. *Factory Farming* (1970); *Man in his living environment* (1970); *Can Britain Survive?* (1971); *The Ethology and Ethics of Farm Animal Production* (1978); *Animals' Rights* (1979).

PROFESSOR SYDNEY JENNINGS Past president of British Veterinary Association. 13 years general mixed practice before teaching at Edinburgh and Glasgow Universities. Formerly director U.N. Project for improvement of veterinary education, Mexico.

REV. ANDREW LINZEY Chaplain/Lecturer, Religious Studies, North East Surrey College of Technology at Ewell. Currently pursuing research into Christian Doctrine of Creation. Publications: *Animal Rights* (1976); contrib. *Animals' Rights - A Symposium* (1979).

THE RT. REV. DR. HUGH MONTEFIORE Bishop of Birmingham; formerly Dean of Caius College, Cambridge; Publications: *Can Man Survive?* (1969); (ed.) *Man and Nature* (1975); *Taking our Past into our Future* (1978).

PROFESSOR W.H.THORPE Emeritus Professor of Animal Ethology, University of Cambridge. Fellow and formerly President, Jesus College, Cambridge. Joint Editor, *Behaviour: an International Journal of Comparative Ethology*. Former President, Association for Study of Animal Behaviour; Society of British Entomology; British Ornithologists Union; Sect.D(Zoology) British Association. Fellow, Royal Society. Former member, "Brambell Committee" (1964-65); Publications: *Learning and Instinct in Animals* (1956); *Biology and the Nature of Man* (1962); *Science, Man and Morals* (1965); *Quakers and Humanists* (1968); *Animal Nature and Human Nature* (1974); *Purpose in a World of Chance* (1978); *The Origins and Rise of Ethology* (1979).